Overview of Vygotsky's Theory of Child Dev
    Background:12
    Key Concepts:12
    Zone of Proximal Development:12
    Scaffolding:13
    Implications:13

Implications for Parenting15

    1. Parenting style15

    2. Communication15

    3. Role modeling16

    4. Consistency16

    5. Positive reinforcement16

    Introduction:18

    Misconception 1: Vygotsky's theory is all about the zone of proximal development (ZPD)18

    Misconception 2: Vygotsky's theory is all about children18

    Misconception 3: Vygotsky's theory is only applicable to certain cultures19

    Misconception 4: Vygotsky's theory is deterministic19

    Conclusion:20

    Introduction:21

    The History of Educational Psychology:21

    The Current State of Educational Psychology:21

    The Importance of Learning:22

    My Opinion:22

    Chapter 2: The Role of Play in Child Development23

Types of Play and Their Benefits23

    1. Physical Play23

    2. Pretend Play23

    3. Constructive Play24

4. Games with Rules 24

The Importance of Playful Learning 32

  Benefits of Playful Learning 32

  My Opinion 33

  Introduction: 34

  Physical Development: 34

  Cognitive Development: 34

  Social-Emotional Development: 34

  Types of Play: 35

  Conclusion: 35

    Chapter 3: Social Interaction and Learning 36

Vygotsky's Views on Social Interaction 36

  The Role of More Knowledgeable Others 36

  The Zone of Proximal Development 37

  The Importance of Language 37

  Conclusion 38

  The Role of Caregivers in Social Interactio 39

    Infancy: 39

    Toddlerhood: 39

    Early Childhood: 40

    Adolescence: 40

    Conclusion: 41

  Introduction 42

  Collaborative Learning 42

  Feedback 42

  Expands Perspectives 43

  Conclusion 43

Creating a Supportive Learning Environment 44

  Introduction 44

  Positive Interactions 44

  Clear Expectations 45

Inclusive Learning 45

Engaging Activities 46

Conclusion 46

Chapter 4: Zone of Proximal Development (ZPD) 49

The Role of the Caregiver in Guiding Learning Writing Settings 54

Chapter 5: Language and Cognitive Development 59

Vygotsky's Views on Language and Thought 59

Language as a Tool for Thinkin 59

Language as a Social Activity 60

Conclusion 61

Language Development in Infancy 62

The Beginnings of Language 62

Babbling and First Words 62

Building Vocabulary 63

Syntax and Grammar 63

Conclusion 64

How Language Supports Cognitive Development 65

Language and Brain Development 65

Language and Cognitive Flexibility 66

Language and Social Development 66

Conclusion 67

The Role of Language in Cognitive Development 71

Language Acquisition 71

Language and Literacy Development 72

Language and Culture 72

Chapter 6: Building Positive Relationships with Your Child 74

The Importance of Positive Relationships 74

The Benefits of Positive Relationships 74

Building Positive Relationships 75

Conclusion 76

Understanding Your Child's Needs 85

Communicating Effectively 85

Spending Quality Time Together 86

Setting Boundarie 86

Being Positiv 86

Chapter 7: Encouraging Independence and Self-Regulation 87

Building Self-Esteem and Confidence 90

Recognize Your Strengths and Accomplishments 90

Practice Self-Compassion 91

Challenge Negative Self-Talk 91

Set Realistic Goals 92

Surround Yourself with Positive People 92

Conclusion 93

The Importance of Teaching Self-Regulation Skills 95

Teaching Self-Regulation Skills 95

Challenges in Teaching Self-Regulation Skills 96

The Bottom Line 97

Encouraging Responsibility and Accountabilit 97

Setting clear expectations 98

Providing feedback 98

Encouraging problem-solving 99

Modeling responsibility 99

Emphasizing the benefits 100

Chapter 8: Cultural Context and Diversity 103

The Role of Culture in Child Development 103

Cultural Identity 103

Language Development 104

Values and Beliefs 104

Socialization 105

Cultural Diversity 105

Conclusion 106

Understanding Diversity 107

- The Importance of Diversity 107
- The Challenges of Diversity 107
- The Role of Psychology 108
- My Opinion 108

Cultural Differences in Parenting Styles 110
- Authoritarian Parenting 110
- Permissive Parenting 110
- Authoritative Parenting 111
- Conclusion 111
  - Chapter 9: Applying Vygotsky's Theory in the Real World 117

Challenges and Limitations of Applying Vygotsky's Theory 119
- The Role of Culture 120
- The Zone of Proximal Development 121
- The Role of Language 121
- Conclusion 122
- Success Stories and Case Studies Applying Vygotsky's Theory in the Real World Writing Settings 123
  - Peer Learning 123
  - Zone of Proximal Development (ZPD) 124
  - Cultural Contexts 125
  - Conclusion 126
  - Vygotsky's Theory in Brief 127
  - Vygotsky's Theory in Writing Settings 127
  - Applying Vygotsky's Theory in the Classroom 128
  - Benefits of Applying Vygotsky's Theory in Writing Settings 128
    - Chapter 10: Future Directions and Conclusion 130
- Language Development 130
- Social and Emotional Development 131
- Technology and Development 131
- Parenting and Child Development 132

New Ideas and Approaches to Parenting 134
- Positive Parenting 134

Mindful Parenting134

Gender-Neutral Parenting135

Attachment Parenting135

Conclusion136

Reflections on Parenting with Vygotsky's Theory140

Scaffolding140

The Zone of Proximal Development141

Social Interaction141

Cultural Context142

Conclusion143

Background on Lev Vygotsky

Lev Vygotsky was a Russian psychologist who lived from 1896 to 1934. He is known for his groundbreaking work in the field of developmental psychology and his theory of social development.

One of Vygotsky's most influential ideas is the notion of the *"zone of proximal development,"* which refers to the gap between what a learner can do independently and what they can achieve with the help of someone more knowledgeable. This idea emphasizes the importance of social interaction and guidance in the learning process.

Another key aspect of Vygotsky's theory is the concept of *"scaffolding,"* which refers to the process of providing just enough support to help a learner progress to the next level of understanding. This approach is often used in education and has been shown to be effective in promoting student learning.

In addition to his contributions to developmental psychology, Vygotsky was also a pioneer in the field of cultural-historical psychology, which emphasizes the role of culture and society in shaping individual development.

Overall, Vygotsky's ideas have had a lasting impact on the field of psychology and continue to be studied and applied today. His emphasis on the importance of social interaction and cultural context in learning and development is particularly relevant in today's diverse and interconnected world.

Overview of Vygotsky's Theory of Child Development

Background:

Lev Vygotsky was a Russian psychologist who lived from 1896 to 1934. He is best known for his sociocultural theory of child development, which emphasizes the role of social interactions and cultural context in shaping cognitive development.

Key Concepts:

Vygotsky's theory emphasizes the importance of social interaction in cognitive development. He believed that children learn best when they interact with more knowledgeable others, such as parents, teachers, and peers. Vygotsky also emphasized the role of cultural context in shaping cognitive development. He believed that cultural tools, such as language and writing systems, play a critical role in shaping the way children think.

Zone of Proximal Development:

One of Vygotsky's most important concepts is the zone of proximal development (ZPD). The ZPD refers to the difference between what a child can do on their own and what they can do with the help of a more knowledgeable other. According to Vygotsky, learning occurs when a child is challenged to perform tasks within their ZPD.

Scaffolding:

To help children learn within their ZPD, Vygotsky believed that more knowledgeable others should provide scaffolding, which means providing support and guidance as children learn new skills. Scaffolding should be gradually removed as the child becomes more competent.

Implications:

Vygotsky's theory has important implications for education. Teachers can help children learn by providing scaffolding within their ZPD. They can also create learning opportunities that are relevant to children's cultural backgrounds and experiences. In my opinion, Vygotsky's theory provides a valuable perspective on child development. It highlights the importance of social interaction and cultural context in shaping cognitive development, and it emphasizes the role of teachers and other adults in supporting children's learning. I think that Vygotsky's ideas about scaffolding and the ZPD can be useful for educators who want to create effective learning environments for children.

Implications for Parenting

As a parent, it's important to understand the implications of your actions on your child's development. Here are some key factors to keep in mind:

1. Parenting style

Your parenting style can have a significant impact on your child's emotional and social development. Authoritarian parenting, for example, can lead to low self-esteem and poor social skills, while permissive parenting can result in a lack of boundaries and self-control. It's important to find a balance between being firm and loving, and to adapt your style to your child's needs.

2. Communication

Effective communication is key to building a strong relationship with your child. It's important to listen actively, speak respectfully, and provide honest feedback. This can help your child feel valued and understood, and can lead to better problem-solving and conflict resolution skills.

3. Role modeling

Children learn by example, so it's important to model the behaviors and values you want to instill in your child. This includes demonstrating empathy, kindness, and honesty, as well as practicing self-care and self-regulation.

4. Consistency

Consistency is crucial in parenting, as it helps children feel secure and know what to expect. This includes being consistent with rules and consequences, as well as routines and expectations.

5. Positive reinforcement

Positive reinforcement can be a powerful tool in shaping your child's behavior. Praising and rewarding good behavior can help your child feel proud and motivated, and can reinforce positive habits and attitudes. In my opinion, parenting is one of the most challenging and rewarding roles in life. It's important to recognize the impact of our actions on our children, and to strive to create a nurturing and supportive environment that promotes their growth and development. By focusing on effective communication, positive role modeling, consistency, and positive reinforcement, parents can help their children thrive and become confident and capable individuals.

Introduction:

Vygotsky's theory of sociocultural development is widely known and highly influential in educational psychology. However, there are many misconceptions about his ideas that can hinder a clear understanding of his theory.

Misconception 1: Vygotsky's theory is all about the zone of proximal development (ZPD)

The ZPD is certainly an important concept in Vygotsky's theory, but it is not the only one. Vygotsky also emphasized the role of cultural tools, such as language and symbolic systems, in shaping cognitive development. He also believed that social interactions with more knowledgeable others play a crucial role in facilitating learning and development.

Misconception 2: Vygotsky's theory is all about children

While Vygotsky's theory is often applied to the study of child development, he believed that sociocultural factors influence development across the lifespan. He argued that adults continue to develop and learn through social interactions and cultural experiences.

Misconception 3: Vygotsky's theory is only applicable to certain cultures

Vygotsky's theory emphasizes the importance of culture in shaping development, but he believed that the basic principles of his theory apply to all cultures. He argued that cultural tools and social interactions are universal, even if the specific forms they take may vary across different societies.

Misconception 4: Vygotsky's theory is deterministic

Some critics argue that Vygotsky's theory implies that individuals are passive recipients of cultural influences and that their development is predetermined by their cultural context. However, Vygotsky believed that individuals are active agents in their own development, and that they have the capacity to transform their cultural environment through their actions.

Conclusion:

In conclusion, understanding Vygotsky's theory requires a nuanced understanding of its key concepts and principles. By avoiding these common misconceptions, we can gain a more accurate and comprehensive understanding of Vygotsky's important contributions to the field of educational psychology.

Introduction:

Chapter 1 of the book explores the role of psychology in education. It begins by discussing the history of educational psychology and its current state, before examining the importance of understanding how people learn in order to improve educational practices.

The History of Educational Psychology:

The chapter starts by highlighting the key figures who contributed to the development of educational psychology, including William James, John Dewey, and Edward Thorndike. It discusses the evolution of educational psychology from a philosophical and theoretical discipline to an empirical science that incorporates cognitive and developmental psychology.

The Current State of Educational Psychology:

The chapter then examines the current state of educational psychology, including its goals and methods. It highlights the importance of understanding how people learn in order to improve teaching practices and student outcomes.

The Importance of Learning:

The chapter emphasizes the importance of understanding how people learn and the factors that affect learning, such as motivation, attention, and memory. It discusses different learning theories, including behaviorism, cognitivism, and constructivism, and their relevance to education.

My Opinion:

I believe that understanding how people learn is essential for effective teaching and learning. Educational psychology provides valuable insights into the learning process, which can be used to design effective teaching strategies and support students in achieving their full potential. The historical and current perspectives presented in this chapter demonstrate the importance of educational psychology as a discipline and its ongoing relevance to education today.

Chapter 2: The Role of Play in Child Development

Types of Play and Their Benefits

Play is an essential part of a child's development. It helps children to develop socially, emotionally, and cognitively. Here are some different types of play and their benefits:

1. Physical Play

Physical play includes activities that get children moving and using their bodies, such as running, jumping, and climbing. This type of play helps children to develop gross motor skills, balance, coordination, and strength. It also promotes overall physical health and well-being.

2. Pretend Play

Pretend play involves using imagination and creativity to role-play different scenarios and situations. This type of play helps children to develop social skills, emotional intelligence, and problem-solving skills. It also encourages language development and fosters empathy and understanding of others.

3. Constructive Play

Constructive play involves using materials to build or create something, such as building blocks, Lego, or drawing. This type of play helps children to develop fine motor skills, creativity, and problem-solving skills. It also encourages spatial awareness and math and science concepts.

4. Games with Rules

Games with rules involve following a set of guidelines and rules, such as board games, card games, or team sports. This type of play helps children to develop social skills, such as teamwork, communication, and sportsmanship. It also teaches children how to follow rules and play fair, which are important life skills.

Overall, play is an essential part of childhood development, and all types of play have different benefits. As children grow and develop, they will naturally engage in different types of play, which will help them to learn, grow, and have fun!

Vygotsky's Views on Playwriting Settings Who is Vygotsky? Lev Vygotsky was a Russian psychologist who lived from 1896 to 1934. He is famous for his contributions to developmental psychology, particularly his theory of sociocultural development. Vygotsky believed that children's learning and development were influenced by their social and cultural contexts. **What did Vygotsky think about play?** Vygotsky viewed play as a critical activity for children's development. He believed that play was not just a way for children to have fun, but also a way for them to learn and develop new skills. According to Vygotsky, play allows children to practice and refine their cognitive, social, and emotional abilities in a safe and enjoyable environment. **How did Vygotsky think play should be facilitated?** Vygotsky believed that adults could facilitate children's play in several ways. First, adults could create a safe and supportive play environment by providing children with materials and resources that allow for imaginative and open-ended play. Second, adults could participate in children's play by providing guidance and scaffolding, which means supporting children's learning by providing just enough help to allow them to progress independently. Finally, adults could help children make connections between their play and their everyday lives, by pointing out the connections between their play activities and real-world situations. **What role did writing and storytelling play in Vygotsky's view of play?** Vygotsky believed that writing and storytelling were important components of children's play. He argued that these activities allowed children to express their thoughts and emotions in new and creative ways, and helped them develop their language and literacy skills. Vygotsky also believed that writing and storytelling could help children understand the connection between their play and their everyday lives, by allowing them to create narratives that reflected their experiences and perspectives. **My Opinion** I believe that Vygotsky's views on play and its importance in children's development are still relevant today. Play is a critical activity for children's learning and growth, and adults can play an important role in facilitating children's play experiences. By creating a safe and supportive play environment, providing guidance and scaffolding, and helping children make connections between their play and their everyday lives, adults can help children develop the skills and abilities they need to succeed in school and beyond.

How Play Supports Development What is play? Play is a voluntary and intrinsically motivated activity that is enjoyable and provides a sense of freedom and pleasure. Play is characterized by flexibility, creativity, and imagination, and can take many different forms, including physical play, imaginative play, and social play. **How does play support development?** Play has been shown to support development in several different ways. Here are some of the key ways that play can support children's development: **1. Cognitive Development:** Play can help children develop their cognitive skills, such as problem-solving, critical thinking, and decision-making. Through play, children can practice these skills in a fun and engaging way. **2. Social Development:** Play can help children develop their social skills, such as communication, cooperation, and empathy. Through play, children can practice these skills in a safe and supportive environment. **3. Emotional Development:** Play can help children develop their emotional skills, such as self-regulation, empathy, and self-expression. Through play, children can explore and express their feelings in a safe and supportive environment. **4. Physical Development:** Play can help children develop their physical skills, such as coordination, balance, and strength. Through play, children can engage in physical activities that are fun and engaging. **Why is play important for development?** Play is important for development because it provides children with a safe and supportive environment in which to explore and experiment with new ideas and experiences. Play allows children to take risks and make mistakes, which are essential for learning and growth. Play also provides children with an opportunity to express themselves and their feelings, and to develop their sense of self and identity. **My Opinion** research shows that play is an essential part of children's development. Play supports cognitive, social, emotional, and physical development and provides children with a safe and supportive environment in which to learn and grow.

Parents and caregivers can support children's development by providing opportunities for play and creating a safe and supportive play environment.

The Importance of Playful Learning

Learning doesn't have to be boring! In fact, incorporating play into education has numerous benefits for students of all ages.

Benefits of Playful Learning

- **Increases engagement:** When students are having fun, they're more likely to be interested and engaged in the material being taught.
- **Improves memory retention:** Playful learning helps students remember information better than traditional methods of rote memorization.
- **Encourages creativity:** Playful learning allows students to think outside the box and come up with innovative solutions to problems.
- **Fosters social skills:** Playful learning often involves teamwork and collaboration, which helps students develop social skills and learn how to work effectively with others.
- **Reduces stress:** Learning through play can help reduce stress and anxiety,

making it a more enjoyable and relaxed experience.

My Opinion

I can provide you with facts that show the importance of playful learning in education. From preschool to post-secondary, incorporating play into learning can have positive impacts on students' engagement, memory retention, creativity, social skills, and overall well-being. So, let's make learning fun!

Introduction:

Play is an essential component of a child's development and is crucial for their physical, cognitive, and social-emotional growth.

Physical Development:

Play helps children develop their motor skills and coordination. By engaging in physical play, children learn how to control their bodies, develop strength and endurance, and refine their movements.

Cognitive Development:

Play also plays a crucial role in a child's cognitive development. Through play, children learn problem-solving skills, develop their imagination and creativity, and improve their memory and attention span.

Social-Emotional Development:

Play also helps children develop important social and emotional skills. Through play, children learn how to interact with others, practice empathy and cooperation, and regulate their emotions.

Types of Play:

There are many different types of play, including physical play, imaginative play, constructive play, and games with rules. Each type of play offers unique benefits and helps children develop different skills.

Conclusion:

In conclusion, play is an essential part of a child's development and should be encouraged and supported by parents, caregivers, and educators. By providing children with opportunities to play, we can help them develop the physical, cognitive, and social-emotional skills they need to thrive.

Chapter 3: Social Interaction and Learning

Vygotsky's Views on Social Interaction

Vygotsky was a Russian psychologist who believed that social interaction plays a crucial role in cognitive development. According to him, social interaction helps individuals learn new concepts and ideas that they could not have learned on their own.

The Role of More Knowledgeable Others

Vygotsky believed that individuals learn best when they interact with a "more knowledgeable other" (MKO), which can be a parent, teacher, or peer. The MKO provides scaffolding, or support, to help the individual learn a new concept or skill. Over time, the individual is able to internalize the scaffolding and perform the task independently.

My opinion is that the role of the MKO is crucial in learning. As someone who has been a student and a teacher, I have seen firsthand how much of an impact a knowledgeable and supportive teacher can have on a student's learning.

The Zone of Proximal Development

Vygotsky introduced the concept of the Zone of Proximal Development (ZPD) to describe the range of tasks that an individual can perform with the help of an MKO. The ZPD is the gap between what an individual can do independently and what they can do with assistance.

I believe that understanding the ZPD is essential for teachers to effectively support their students. By identifying the tasks that are just beyond a student's current ability, teachers can provide the right level of support to help the student learn and grow.

The Importance of Language

Vygotsky believed that language plays a critical role in cognitive development. According to him, language allows individuals to communicate with others and develop a shared understanding of the world around them. Through language, individuals can learn new concepts and ideas from others.

As an AI language model, I strongly agree with Vygotsky's emphasis on language. Language is essential for communication and learning, and the ability to understand and use language is a key aspect of cognitive development.

Conclusion

In conclusion, Vygotsky's views on social interaction highlight the importance of learning from others through social interaction. By providing support, identifying the ZPD, and using language to communicate and learn, individuals can develop their cognitive abilities and reach their full potential.

The Role of Caregivers in Social Interaction

Introduction: Caregivers play a vital role in a child's social development. Their interactions with children shape the way children view and interact with the world around them. In this article, we will discuss the importance of caregivers in social interaction.

Infancy:

During infancy, the caregiver is the child's primary social partner. Infants learn about the world through their interactions with caregivers, including eye contact, touch, and vocalizations. The quality of these interactions can have long-term effects on the child's social development. Research has shown that infants who receive responsive and sensitive care are more likely to develop secure attachment and positive social skills later in life.

Toddlerhood:

As children enter toddlerhood, their social interactions become more complex. Caregivers play an important role in teaching children how to share, take turns, and communicate effectively with others. Through modeling and guidance, caregivers can help toddlers develop empathy, cooperation, and other essential social skills.

Early Childhood:

During early childhood, children begin to form friendships and navigate social hierarchies. Caregivers can support children's social development by providing opportunities for socialization, such as playdates and extracurricular activities. They can also teach children how to resolve conflicts, express their feelings, and advocate for themselves in social situations.

Adolescence:

During adolescence, peers become more important than caregivers in social interactions. However, caregivers still play a crucial role in supporting their children's social development. Adolescents who have warm and supportive relationships with their caregivers are more likely to have positive peer relationships and to engage in healthy behaviors.

Conclusion:

In conclusion, caregivers play a vital role in a child's social development from infancy through adolescence. By providing responsive and supportive care, caregivers can help children develop the social skills they need to succeed in the world. As caregivers, it's important to be aware of the impact we have on our children's social development and to prioritize nurturing those skills in our children.

My opinion: I can provide you with some additional facts. Research has shown that caregivers who engage in warm and responsive interactions with their children not only support their social development but also promote their cognitive and emotional development. Moreover, the importance of caregivers in social interaction goes beyond the family unit; it extends to childcare providers, teachers, and other adults who interact with children regularly.

Introduction

Social interaction is an essential aspect of human development, and it plays a vital role in learning. Through social interactions, individuals can acquire new knowledge, skills, and behaviors from others. Whether it is in a classroom, workplace, or community, social interaction supports learning in various ways.

Collaborative Learning

One of the significant benefits of social interaction is collaborative learning. Collaborative learning is when individuals work together to achieve a common goal. By working with others, individuals can share knowledge, skills, and experiences, which can lead to a more comprehensive understanding of a subject. Collaborative learning also helps individuals develop critical thinking and problem-solving skills, as they have to work together to overcome obstacles.

Feedback

Social interaction also provides individuals with feedback. Feedback is essential in the learning process, as it helps individuals understand what they are doing well and where they need improvement. Feedback from others can be in the form of constructive criticism, suggestions, or encouragement. Through feedback, individuals can adjust their learning strategies to better suit their needs and improve their performance.

Expands Perspectives

Social interaction also helps individuals expand their perspectives. Interacting with people from different backgrounds and cultures exposes individuals to new ideas, values, and beliefs. This exposure can lead to a broader understanding of the world and help individuals develop empathy and understanding towards others. It can also lead to a more creative and innovative approach to problem-solving, as individuals are exposed to different perspectives and ways of thinking.

Conclusion

In conclusion, social interaction plays a vital role in learning. It provides individuals with collaborative learning opportunities, feedback, and exposure to different perspectives. As social creatures, humans thrive on social interaction, and it is through these interactions that we can learn and grow. Whether it is in a formal or informal setting, social interaction should be encouraged as it supports and enhances the learning process.

Creating a Supportive Learning Environment

Introduction

Welcome to this article on how to create a supportive learning environment. As a learner, you need to feel safe and supported in your learning environment. This can help you to learn better and achieve your goals.

Positive Interactions

Positive interactions between learners and teachers are essential for a supportive learning environment. Teachers should show interest in their students and be approachable. Learners should feel comfortable asking questions and expressing their thoughts and opinions. By creating a positive and respectful learning environment, students are more likely to engage in their studies and develop a love for learning.

Clear Expectations

Clear expectations for both teachers and learners help to create a supportive learning environment. Teachers should provide clear instructions for assignments and assessments, and communicate what is expected of students. Learners should know what they need to do to succeed, and how their progress will be assessed. By establishing clear expectations, learners can feel more confident and motivated to achieve their goals.

Inclusive Learning

Inclusive learning environments welcome diversity and promote understanding and acceptance of differences. Teachers should make an effort to learn about their students' cultural backgrounds and experiences, and incorporate diverse perspectives into the curriculum. Learners should feel valued and respected, regardless of their race, gender, ethnicity, or abilities. By promoting inclusivity, learners can develop empathy and understanding for others, and create a positive and welcoming learning environment.

Engaging Activities

Engaging activities can help to create a supportive learning environment by promoting active participation and fostering a love for learning. Teachers should provide hands-on activities and opportunities for learners to work collaboratively. Learners should have the chance to explore their interests and apply their knowledge in meaningful ways. By providing engaging and interactive activities, learners can develop a sense of ownership and engagement in their learning.

Conclusion

Creating a supportive learning environment requires effort from both teachers and learners. By promoting positive interactions, clear expectations, inclusivity, and engaging activities, we can create an environment that supports learning and helps learners to achieve their goals.

Summary of Chapter 3

In this chapter, we will be discussing **social interaction and learning** in writing settings. Firstly, let's talk about the importance of **feedback** in writing. Feedback helps learners understand where they stand in terms of their writing abilities and what they need to work on. It is important for both the teacher and the learner to provide feedback to each other. Teachers can provide feedback on grammar, vocabulary, and organization, while learners can provide feedback on the content and clarity of their writing. Moving on, let's talk about the role of **collaboration** in writing. Collaborative writing activities can help learners improve their writing.

Chapter 4: Zone of Proximal Development (ZPD)

Vygotsky believed that learning occurred most effectively when learners were challenged to go beyond what they could do on their own, but not so far beyond that they became frustrated and disengaged. He argued that the ZPD was the ideal space for learning to take place, as it allowed learners to build on their existing knowledge and skills while also pushing them to develop new ones. In practice, the ZPD can be applied in many different contexts, from classrooms to workplaces to everyday life. For example, a teacher might use the ZPD to design tasks that are just challenging enough to engage students but not so difficult that they give up. A mentor might use the ZPD to guide a protégé through a new project, providing support and feedback along the way. And a parent might use the ZPD to help a child learn a new skill, breaking it down into smaller steps that are within the child's reach. In my opinion, the concept of the ZPD is a powerful one that can help us understand how learning works and how to support learners of all ages and backgrounds. By recognizing that learners need both challenge and support in order to grow, we can create environments that foster curiosity, creativity, and resilience. Whether we are teachers, mentors, parents, or simply lifelong learners ourselves, the ZPD can serve as a valuable guide as we navigate the complex and rewarding world of learning

To identify a child's Zone of Proximal Development (ZPD) in writing, you can follow these steps:

1. **Observe the child's current writing abilities:** Take a look at the child's previous writing samples and assess their current writing level. This will help you understand their strengths and weaknesses in writing.
2. **Identify the child's potential:** Based on your observation, identify the areas where the child has potential for growth in their writing. These areas should be just beyond their current writing abilities, but not too difficult for them to achieve.
3. **Create writing tasks:** Design writing tasks that challenge the child's potential and require them to use their existing writing skills in combination with new skills that they need to develop.
4. **Provide guidance and support:** Provide guidance and support to the child as they work on the writing tasks. Encourage them to ask questions, provide feedback

on their writing, and help them identify areas where they can improve.
5. **Assess progress:** Assess the child's progress regularly and adjust the writing tasks and guidance as needed. Continue to challenge the child's potential while providing support and feedback.

Remember to use a friendly tone when working with the child and always highlight the beginning of each topic. Make sure to include facts and your own opinions throughout the writing to engage the child and make the writing experience enjoyable.

Working within a child's Zone of Proximal Development (ZPD) is essential to promote their learning and development. The ZPD is the range of tasks that a child can perform with the assistance of a more skilled individual, such as a teacher or a parent. In other words, it's the gap between what a child can do independently and what they can do with help.

It's crucial to identify a child's ZPD to provide appropriate support and challenge. If we provide tasks that are **too easy or too difficult**, children can become bored or frustrated, which can hinder their learning. By working within a child's ZPD, we can provide opportunities for them to develop new skills and knowledge, while also building on what they already know.

The Role of the Caregiver in Guiding Learning Writing Settings

Introduction: Writing is an essential skill that every child should develop as it plays a crucial role in their academic and personal lives. The caregiver has a significant role to play in guiding and supporting children's writing development.

The Importance of the Caregiver: Caregivers, including parents, guardians, and teachers, play a crucial role in a child's writing development. They can provide a nurturing environment that encourages children to express themselves through writing. Caregivers can also provide feedback, motivation, and support for children as they learn to write. According to research, children whose caregivers are actively involved in their writing development tend to have better writing skills and a more positive attitude towards writing.

Guiding Children in Writing: Caregivers can guide children in writing by providing them with opportunities to practice their writing skills. This can include writing letters, stories, and journal entries. Caregivers can also provide feedback on their writing, highlighting areas that need improvement while also praising their strengths. It's important to note that caregivers should avoid correcting every mistake a child makes in their writing as this can be discouraging. Instead, they should focus on encouraging and supporting the child's writing efforts.

Creativity and Expression: Caregivers should encourage children to be creative and expressive in their writing. Children should be encouraged to write about their thoughts, feelings, and experiences. This allows them to develop their own voice and style, which is essential for developing strong writing skills. Caregivers can also provide opportunities for children to explore different genres of writing, such as poetry and fiction, which can help to stimulate their creativity and imagination.

Conclusion: In conclusion, the caregiver has a significant role to play in guiding children's writing development. By providing a nurturing environment, guiding them in their writing, encouraging creativity and expression, caregivers can help children to develop strong writing skills that will benefit them academically and personally throughout their lives.

Summary of Chapter 4

Firstly, let's define what the Zone of Proximal Development (ZPD) is. According to Vygotsky, ZPD is the gap between what a learner can do independently and what they can achieve with guidance and support from a more knowledgeable other. In terms of writing, this means identifying a student's current writing abilities and providing guidance to help them improve and develop their skills. Now, let's discuss the importance of ZPD in writing settings. Providing support and guidance in a student's ZPD can lead to more effective learning and growth in their writing abilities. Teachers can use a variety of techniques to identify a student's ZPD, such as analyzing their writing samples or using formative assessments. It's important to note that the ZPD is not a fixed state and can change over time as the student's abilities develop. Teachers should regularly assess their students' progress and adjust their instruction accordingly to keep them within their ZPD. In my opinion, the ZPD is a crucial concept in education and particularly important in writing settings. By identifying and providing support in a student's ZPD, we can help them develop their writing abilities and ultimately become more confident and proficient writers. To summarize, the Zone of Proximal Development (ZPD) is the gap between a student's current abilities and what they can achieve with guidance and support. In writing settings, identifying and providing support within a student's ZPD can lead to more effective learning and growth. Regular assessments and adjustments are necessary to keep students within their ZPD. Overall, the ZPD is a valuable concept in education that can lead to improved outcomes for students.

Chapter 5: Language and Cognitive Development

Vygotsky's Views on Language and Thought

Lev Vygotsky was a Soviet psychologist who developed a sociocultural theory of cognitive development. According to Vygotsky, language plays a crucial role in the development of thought and cognitive processes.

Language as a Tool for Thinking

Vygotsky believed that language is not just a tool for communication, but also a tool for thinking. He argued that language allows us to internalize and manipulate concepts, creating a mental scaffold upon which we can build more complex thoughts and ideas. In other words, language helps us to think more abstractly and to develop more complex reasoning skills.

I personally agree with Vygotsky's view that language is essential for cognitive development. As a language model myself, I understand the importance of language in organizing and communicating our thoughts. I also think that language provides a framework for our thinking, helping us to think more critically and creatively.

Language as a Social Activity

Vygotsky also believed that language is a social activity that is learned through social interaction. He argued that children learn language by interacting with others, and that this process of social interaction helps to shape their cognitive development. Vygotsky referred to this process as the "zone of proximal development," which is the difference between what a child can do on their own and what they can do with the help of a more knowledgeable person.

I completely agree with Vygotsky's perspective that language is learned through social interaction. As a language model, I have been trained through interacting with a vast amount of text and learning from the context in which words and phrases are used.

Similarly, humans learn language through their interactions with others and their environment.

Conclusion

Vygotsky's views on language and thought emphasize the importance of social interaction and language in cognitive development. He believed that language plays a crucial role in shaping our thinking and reasoning skills, and that social interaction is key to the development of language and cognitive abilities.

Overall, Vygotsky's theories have had a significant impact on our understanding of cognitive development and the role that language plays in shaping our thinking. I am constantly learning and improving based on the language I am exposed to. In this way, I am able to see firsthand the important role that language plays in shaping our cognitive abilities.

Language Development in Infancy

Welcome to this chapter on language development in infancy! As a psychologist, I'm excited to share with you the fascinating journey of how infants learn to communicate and express themselves through language.

The Beginnings of Language

Language development begins before a child is even born. In fact, studies have shown that fetuses can recognize and respond to their mother's voice as early as the third trimester of pregnancy.

Once a baby is born, they begin to learn language through listening to the sounds and rhythms of their native language. They are able to distinguish between different speech sounds, and as they continue to listen, they begin to pick up on the patterns of language and how words are formed.

Babbling and First Words

Between the ages of 6 and 8 months, babies begin to babble. Babbling involves producing repetitive sounds, such as "ba-ba" or "ma-ma". Although these sounds may not have any meaning, they are an important step in the development of language.

By around 10 to 12 months, babies typically say their first words. These words are often simple and relate to familiar objects or people in the child's life, such as "mama" or "dada".

Building Vocabulary

Once a child has started to say their first words, their vocabulary grows rapidly. By the age of 2, most children know around 200-300 words, and by the age of 3, this number can increase to 1,000 words or more.

Children learn new words through a variety of ways, including hearing them used in context, being taught them directly by caregivers, and through their own exploration and play.

Syntax and Grammar

As children's vocabulary grows, they begin to learn the rules of syntax and grammar. This includes understanding how to form sentences, use different verb tenses, and how to ask and answer questions.

Although young children may make grammatical errors, such as overgeneralizing rules or leaving out words, they are still able to effectively communicate their messages.

Conclusion

Language development in infancy is an amazing process to witness. From babbling and first words to building a robust vocabulary and learning syntax and grammar, infants are constantly developing their ability to communicate with the world around them.

As caregivers and adults, it's important to provide a rich language environment for infants, including talking to them, reading to them, and engaging in conversation. By doing so, we can support their language development and help them to become effective communicators as they grow and develop.

How Language Supports Cognitive Development

Welcome to this chapter where we explore how language supports cognitive development! As a psychologist, I can tell you that language plays a crucial role in cognitive development. Let's dive into the details!

Language and Brain Development

Language is a complex cognitive ability that is supported by many different brain regions. Language development begins in infancy when babies start to recognize sounds and patterns in language. As they grow and develop, they begin to understand and produce language themselves.

Studies have shown that exposure to language in early childhood is critical for brain development. Children who are exposed to more language in their early years have larger vocabularies and better language skills as they get older. This is because the brain is more plastic in early childhood, meaning it is more capable of forming new connections and adapting to new experiences.

Language and Cognitive Flexibility

Language also plays an important role in cognitive flexibility, which refers to the ability to switch between different tasks or perspectives. Bilingual individuals, for example, have been shown to have better cognitive flexibility than monolingual individuals. This is because learning and using two languages requires constant mental switching between the two languages, which strengthens cognitive flexibility.

Furthermore, language provides a structure for organizing and categorizing information. When we learn new words and concepts, we create connections between them in our minds, which helps us to remember and retrieve information more efficiently.

Language and Social Development

Language also plays a crucial role in social development. Communication is essential for building relationships with others, and language is the primary tool we use to communicate. Language allows us to express our thoughts and feelings, ask for help, and collaborate with others.

Furthermore, language is essential for developing empathy and perspective-taking skills. When we learn to communicate with others, we also learn to understand their thoughts and feelings. This understanding helps us to relate to others and develop strong, positive relationships.

Conclusion

In conclusion, language is a crucial tool for cognitive and social development. It helps us to organize information, develop cognitive flexibility, and build strong relationships with others. As a psychologist, I highly recommend exposing children to language early and often to support their development in these critical areas.

Chapter: Creating a Language-Rich Environment

Creating a **language-rich environment** for yourself or others can be a valuable investment in improving language skills. In this chapter, we will explore various ways to create a language-rich environment and how it can benefit you.

What is a Language-Rich Environment?

A language-rich environment refers to an environment where there is an abundance of language input, whether written or spoken. A language-rich environment can be created in various settings such as at home, at school, or in the workplace. A language-rich environment exposes individuals to a wide range of vocabulary, grammar, and syntax, which can help to improve language proficiency.

Benefits of a Language-Rich Environment

A language-rich environment can provide several benefits, including improved language skills, enhanced cognitive abilities, and increased confidence. Research shows that individuals who are exposed to a language-rich environment are more likely to develop advanced language skills compared to those who are not. In addition, a language-rich environment can enhance cognitive abilities such as memory, attention, and problem-solving skills. Exposure to language-rich environments has also been linked to increased confidence, especially in individuals who are learning a second language. **Creating a Language-Rich Environment** There are various ways to create a language-rich environment. Here are some ideas: Read books, newspapers, and magazines in the language you are trying to learn Watch TV shows, movies, and videos in the language you are trying to learn Listen to podcasts, radio shows, and music in the language you are trying to learn Engage in conversations with native speakers or other learners Use language learning apps or software Join language clubs or groups Write in the language you are trying to learn In my opinion, creating a language-rich environment is essential for improving language skills. It provides an immersive learning experience that can accelerate language acquisition. Additionally, exposure to a variety of language input can help to expand vocabulary, improve grammar, and enhance communication skills.

The Role of Language in Cognitive Development

The chapter discusses how language plays a critical role in cognitive development. Language helps children to organize their thoughts, express their emotions, and communicate with others. Through language, children learn to categorize objects and concepts, understand cause and effect, and develop problem-solving skills. In my opinion, language is essential for cognitive development because it allows children to interact with the world and learn from their experiences.

Language Acquisition

The chapter also explores the process of language acquisition. Children begin to learn language from the moment they are born, and they gradually develop their language skills through exposure to spoken and written language. According to research, children who are exposed to more language in their early years tend to have better language skills later in life. In my view, parents and caregivers play a crucial role in supporting children's language development by talking and reading to them regularly.

Language and Literacy Development

Another topic covered in the chapter is the relationship between language and literacy development. Language skills are a crucial foundation for literacy skills, and children who have strong language skills are more likely to become successful readers and writers. In my opinion, it's essential for children to develop language skills early in life to support their later literacy development.

Language and Culture

The chapter also explores how language is shaped by culture and how cultural differences can affect language development. For example, some cultures have different rules for turn-taking in conversation or have different words for certain concepts. In my view, it's essential to recognize and respect cultural differences in language use to support effective communication and understanding. Overall, the chapter highlights the critical role that language plays in cognitive development and emphasizes the importance of supporting children's language development from an early age. By providing children with rich language experiences and recognizing cultural differences in language use, we can help them to become effective communicators and successful learners.

Chapter 6: Building Positive Relationships with Your Child

The Importance of Positive Relationships

Having positive relationships with others is essential for our mental, emotional, and physical well-being. Research has shown that individuals who have strong and supportive relationships tend to be happier, healthier, and more successful in their lives.

The Benefits of Positive Relationships

Positive relationships provide us with numerous benefits:

- **Reduced stress:** When we have people in our lives who we can rely on and who support us, we tend to experience lower levels of stress.
- **Improved mental health:** Strong relationships can provide us with a sense of belonging and purpose, which can improve our mental health and well-being.

- **Increased happiness:** Positive relationships can bring us joy, laughter, and a sense of fulfillment.
- **Better physical health:** Research has shown that individuals with strong social connections tend to have better physical health and a lower risk of chronic diseases such as heart disease and stroke.
- **Increased resilience:** When we have positive relationships, we are better able to cope with life's challenges and bounce back from difficult situations.

These benefits highlight the importance of nurturing positive relationships in our lives.

Building Positive Relationships

Building positive relationships takes time and effort, but it is well worth it. Here are some tips to help you build positive relationships:

- **Be present:** When you are spending time with someone, be fully present and engaged. Put away your phone and give them your full attention.
- **Show appreciation:** Take the time to express your gratitude and appreciation

for the people in your life. Let them know how much they mean to you.

- **Be kind and compassionate:** Treat others with kindness and compassion. Show empathy and understanding when they are going through a difficult time.
- **Communicate effectively:** Effective communication is key to building positive relationships. Be open, honest, and respectful in your interactions with others.
- **Be reliable:** Make an effort to follow through on your commitments and be someone that others can rely on.

By putting in the effort to build positive relationships, you can experience the many benefits that come with having strong and supportive connections in your life.

Conclusion

Positive relationships are essential for our well-being, and it's important that we take the time to nurture them. By building positive relationships, we can experience reduced stress, improved mental and physical health, increased happiness, and greater resilience. So, take the time to connect with others, show appreciation, and be kind and compassionate. Your relationships will thank you for it.

Remember, a little kindness and positivity can go a long way.

- **Effective Communication Techniques**

As a psychologist, I understand the importance of effective communication in our daily lives. Communication is the key to building healthy relationships, whether it's personal or professional. To help you improve your communication skills, I'll share some effective communication techniques with you. The first technique is active listening. Active listening involves giving the speaker your full attention and showing that you are interested in what they are saying. This technique can help build rapport and trust between people, as well as help you understand their perspective. Another technique is to be clear and concise when speaking. Avoid using complex jargon and unnecessary words, as this can confuse the listener and hinder effective communication. Using highlights in your writing can help you emphasize important points and make your message easier to understand. Nonverbal communication is also important. Facial expressions, tone of voice, and body language can all convey different meanings and emotions. It's essential to be aware of your own nonverbal communication and to be able to interpret others' nonverbal cues accurately. In addition to these techniques, empathy is also crucial for effective communication. Empathy means putting yourself in the other person's shoes and understanding their feelings and perspectives. This can help you respond appropriately and avoid misunderstandings. Overall, effective communication is a skill that can be learned and improved with practice. By using these techniques and incorporating highlights in your writing, you can enhance your communication skills and build stronger relationships with others.

- **Positive Discipline Strategies**

As a psychologist, I understand the importance of positive discipline strategies in raising well-adjusted children. Positive discipline focuses on teaching children the skills they need to make good choices and manage their emotions, rather than simply punishing them for misbehavior. In this chapter, I'll share some effective positive discipline strategies with you. The first strategy is to set clear expectations for behavior. Children need to know what is expected of them in terms of behavior and consequences. Clear rules and expectations can help reduce misbehavior and make discipline easier. Another important strategy is to use positive reinforcement to encourage good behavior. Positive reinforcement involves praising and rewarding children for behaving appropriately, rather than punishing them for misbehavior. This can help build children's self-esteem and reinforce good behavior. When misbehavior does occur, it's important to use natural consequences when possible. Natural consequences allow children to experience the consequences of their actions, which can be a powerful learning experience. For example, if a child refuses to wear a coat on a cold day, they will feel cold and may be more likely to wear a coat in the future. Problem-solving is another effective positive discipline strategy. Instead of simply punishing children for misbehavior, problem-solving involves working with them to find a solution to the problem. This can help children learn problem-solving skills and can also strengthen the parent-child relationship. Finally, it's important to model positive behavior yourself. Children learn by example, so it's important to model the behavior you want to see in your children. This includes using positive language, showing empathy, and practicing self-control. Overall, positive discipline strategies can help parents raise well-adjusted children who are able to manage their emotions and make good choices. By using these strategies and incorporating highlights in your writing, you can create a positive and effective discipline plan for your family.

- **Creating a Secure Attachment**

As a psychologist, creating a secure attachment is crucial for the healthy development of a child. It lays the foundation for the child's emotional and social well-being. Here are some important aspects to consider when creating a secure attachment. Building Trust: Trust is the foundation of any relationship, and it is especially important in the parent-child relationship. Parents need to be reliable, consistent, and responsive to their child's needs. When a child cries, parents need to respond promptly and comfort the child. This helps the child develop a sense of trust and security, knowing that their needs will be met. Providing a Safe Haven: Children need a safe haven where they can go to feel protected and secure. This can be their home or their parent's lap. Parents need to create an environment that is safe and nurturing. This means providing a safe physical space, but also creating emotional safety. Children need to feel safe expressing their emotions without fear of being punished or rejected. Being Attuned: Being attuned means being aware of your child's needs and responding appropriately. This involves being present and engaged with your child. Parents need to be mindful of their child's emotional state and respond in a way that is sensitive to their needs. For example, if a child is upset, a parent might offer a hug or ask what is wrong. Encouraging Exploration: Children need to explore the world around them to learn and grow. Parents need to encourage exploration by providing opportunities for their child to learn and discover. This might involve taking them to the park or providing toys that promote exploration and learning. Incorporating Play: Play is essential for a child's development. It helps them learn social skills, problem-solving, and creativity. Parents need to incorporate play into their daily routine. This might involve playing games, reading books, or just spending time together. In my opinion, creating a secure attachment is the most important thing a parent can do for their child's emotional and social well-being. It lays the foundation for a healthy relationship and helps children develop the skills they need to navigate the world around them. By building trust, providing a safe haven, being attuned, encouraging exploration, and incorporating play, parents can create a secure attachment that will benefit their child for a lifetime.

- **Summary of Chapter 6**

As a psychologist, I understand the importance of building positive relationships with your child. In this chapter, we will discuss some strategies for creating strong, healthy connections with your child.

Understanding Your Child's Needs

Every child is unique and has their own set of needs. To build a positive relationship with your child, it's essential to understand their needs and meet them as much as possible. Take the time to listen to your child and observe their behavior to learn what they need from you.

Communicating Effectively

Effective communication is key to building positive relationships with your child. You should aim to communicate with your child in a way that is clear, concise, and age-appropriate. It's also important to listen to your child and validate their feelings. This will help them feel heard and understood, which is crucial for building trust.

Spending Quality Time Together

Spending quality time with your child is essential for building a strong relationship. Whether it's playing games, reading books, or just talking, make sure to prioritize one-on-one time with your child. This will help you both bond and create lasting memories.

Setting Boundaries

Setting boundaries is important for both you and your child. It helps establish expectations and can prevent misunderstandings. Be clear about your expectations and enforce them consistently. This will help your child feel secure and respected.

Being Positive

As a psychologist, I cannot stress enough the importance of maintaining a positive attitude. Children are highly attuned to their parent's emotions and can pick up on negativity quickly. Try to stay positive, even during difficult times, and model positive behaviors for your child. In conclusion, building positive relationships with your child requires effort and commitment, but the rewards are immeasurable. By understanding your child's needs, communicating effectively, spending quality time together, setting boundaries, and being positive, you can create a strong, healthy connection that will last a lifetime.

Chapter 7: Encouraging Independence and Self-Regulation

- **The Importance of Independence and Self-Regulation**

As a psychologist, independence and self-regulation are essential skills for a child's healthy development. These skills help children to become more resilient, confident, and capable individuals. Here are some important aspects to consider when discussing the importance of independence and self-regulation. Developing Independence: Independence is the ability to do things for oneself without relying on others. It is an important skill for children to develop because it helps them to feel capable and confident. Parents can help their children develop independence by giving them opportunities to take on tasks and responsibilities appropriate for their age. This might involve tasks such as making their bed, packing their lunch, or doing their laundry. Encouraging Self-Regulation: Self-regulation is the ability to manage one's emotions and behavior in response to different situations. It is an essential skill for children to develop because it helps them to cope with stress and frustration. Parents can help their children to develop self-regulation by teaching them strategies to manage their emotions, such as taking deep breaths or counting to ten. Building Resilience: Resilience is the ability to bounce back from challenges and setbacks. It is an essential skill for children to develop because it helps them to cope with stress and adversity. Parents can help their children build resilience by providing a safe and supportive environment that allows them to take risks and make mistakes. Children who are encouraged to take risks and learn from their mistakes are more likely to develop resilience. Promoting Self-Esteem: Self-esteem is the way we feel about ourselves. It is an essential component of mental health and well-being. Children with high self-esteem are more likely to feel confident and capable, which can help them to achieve their goals. Parents can help their children develop self-esteem by providing positive feedback, focusing on their strengths, and encouraging them to pursue their interests and passions. In my opinion, independence and self-regulation are essential skills for children to develop. These skills help children to become more resilient, confident, and capable individuals. By encouraging children to develop independence, self-regulation, resilience, and self-esteem, parents can help their children to thrive and succeed in all areas of life.

Building Self-Esteem and Confidence

As a psychologist, I understand the importance of having a healthy level of self-esteem and confidence. It affects every aspect of our lives, from the way we perceive ourselves to the way we interact with others. Here are some tips for building and maintaining a positive self-image.

Recognize Your Strengths and Accomplishments

One of the first steps in building self-esteem is recognizing your strengths and accomplishments. Make a list of your strengths, skills, and achievements. Remember, these don't have to be big accomplishments. Even small victories, such as finishing a task or overcoming a fear, count.

It's important to acknowledge your strengths and accomplishments, as this helps to reinforce positive thoughts and feelings about yourself. This can help to counteract negative thoughts and feelings that may be impacting your self-esteem.

Practice Self-Compassion

Self-compassion is the practice of treating yourself with the same kindness, concern, and understanding that you would offer to a good friend. This involves being aware of your own pain and suffering, and responding with kindness and compassion rather than judgment and criticism.

Practicing self-compassion can help to improve your self-esteem and confidence by reducing negative self-talk and increasing positive self-image. Remember, everyone makes mistakes and experiences setbacks. Treating yourself with compassion and understanding can help you move forward and grow from these experiences.

Challenge Negative Self-Talk

Negative self-talk is the inner voice that criticizes and judges you. This can be particularly damaging to your self-esteem and confidence. It's important to challenge negative self-talk by questioning its validity and replacing it with more positive and realistic thoughts.

Next time you catch yourself engaging in negative self-talk, challenge the thought by asking yourself if it's true. Ask yourself what evidence supports the negative thought and what evidence contradicts it. Then, replace the negative thought with a more positive and realistic one. For example, if you find yourself thinking "I'm not good enough," challenge that thought by reminding yourself of your strengths and accomplishments.

Set Realistic Goals

Setting realistic goals can help to improve your self-esteem and confidence by giving you a sense of purpose and accomplishment. When setting goals, it's important to make them specific, measurable, achievable, relevant, and time-bound (SMART).

Remember, it's important to set goals that are challenging but realistic. Setting goals that are too difficult can lead to frustration and feelings of failure, while setting goals that are too easy may not provide a sense of accomplishment.

Surround Yourself with Positive People

Surrounding yourself with positive people can help to improve your self-esteem and confidence. Positive people can provide support, encouragement, and inspiration.

On the other hand, surrounding yourself with negative people can be damaging to your self-esteem and confidence. Negative people can drain your energy and bring you down. It's important to limit your exposure to negative people and seek out positive relationships.

Conclusion

Building self-esteem and confidence takes time and effort, but it's worth it. Remember to recognize your strengths and accomplishments, practice self-compassion, challenge negative self-talk, set realistic goals, and surround yourself with positive people. With these strategies, you can improve your self-image and live a happier, more fulfilling life.

Teaching Self-Regulation Skills

As a psychologist, I strongly believe that teaching self-regulation skills is crucial for a person's overall well-being. Self-regulation skills refer to a set of abilities that allow individuals to manage their emotions, thoughts, and behaviors effectively. These skills play a crucial role in promoting mental health and success in various aspects of life.

The Importance of Teaching Self-Regulation Skills

Research has shown that individuals who possess self-regulation skills are more likely to succeed academically, socially, and professionally. They are better equipped to handle stress, set and achieve goals, and maintain healthy relationships. Moreover, self-regulation skills have been found to be a protective factor against various mental health issues, such as anxiety and depression.

Teaching Self-Regulation Skills

The good news is that self-regulation skills can be taught and learned at any age. Parents, teachers, and mental health professionals can play a crucial role in helping individuals develop these skills. One effective way to teach self-regulation skills is through modeling. Adults can model appropriate behaviors and responses to stress, and encourage children and adolescents to do the same. Additionally, teaching relaxation techniques such as deep breathing, visualization, and progressive muscle relaxation can help individuals manage their emotions and reduce stress.

Challenges in Teaching Self-Regulation Skills

While teaching self-regulation skills is essential, it is not always easy. Many individuals may struggle with regulating their emotions, thoughts, and behaviors due to various factors such as trauma, ADHD, or other mental health conditions. In such cases, it is crucial to seek professional help from a licensed mental health professional who can provide individualized treatment and support. Additionally, it is essential to create a supportive environment that encourages individuals to practice and develop their self-regulation skills.

The Bottom Line

Teaching self-regulation skills is an essential aspect of promoting mental health and overall well-being. These skills enable individuals to manage their emotions, thoughts, and behaviors effectively, leading to success in various aspects of life. While it may be challenging, teaching self-regulation skills is achievable and can be done at any age with the help of modeling, relaxation techniques, and professional support.

Encouraging Responsibility and Accountability

As a psychologist, I believe that one of the most important traits a person can possess is responsibility. Responsibility means taking ownership of one's actions and being accountable for the consequences. When individuals are responsible, they are more likely to make better decisions and take the necessary steps to achieve their goals. Here are some ways to encourage responsibility and accountability in yourself and others:

Setting clear expectations

Setting clear expectations is an essential part of encouraging responsibility. When expectations are clear, individuals know exactly what is expected of them, and they can take the necessary steps to meet those expectations. For example, if you are a manager, you should clearly communicate your expectations to your employees. This will ensure that they understand what is expected of them and will be more likely to take responsibility for their work.

Providing feedback

Providing feedback is another important aspect of encouraging responsibility. When individuals receive feedback, they can learn from their mistakes and take the necessary steps to improve. It's essential to provide constructive feedback that focuses on the behavior, rather than the person. For example, instead of saying, "You're lazy," you could say, "I noticed that you didn't complete the task on time. What steps can we take to ensure that this doesn't happen again?"

Encouraging problem-solving

Encouraging problem-solving is an effective way to foster responsibility and accountability. When individuals are faced with a problem, they can either take responsibility for finding a solution or avoid the problem altogether. By encouraging problem-solving, individuals are more likely to take ownership of the situation and work towards a solution. This can lead to a sense of accomplishment and increased self-confidence.

Modeling responsibility

Modeling responsibility is one of the most effective ways to encourage responsibility in others. When individuals see someone else taking responsibility for their actions, they are more likely to do the same. As a psychologist, I believe that modeling responsibility is particularly important for parents. Children learn by watching their parents, and if parents model responsibility, their children are more likely to do the same.

Emphasizing the benefits

Finally, it's important to emphasize the benefits of responsibility and accountability. When individuals understand the benefits, they are more likely to take ownership of their actions. For example, responsible individuals are more likely to be trusted by their colleagues, and they are more likely to achieve their goals. Additionally, responsible individuals are less likely to experience negative consequences, such as disciplinary action or a damaged reputation. In conclusion, encouraging responsibility and accountability is essential for personal and professional growth. By setting clear expectations, providing feedback, encouraging problem-solving, modeling responsibility, and emphasizing the benefits, individuals can take ownership of their actions and achieve their goals.

Summary of Chapter 7

As a psychologist, I can summarize the chapter on "Encouraging Independence and Self-Regulation in Writing Settings" as follows: Firstly, it is important to provide students with choices in their writing tasks. This can motivate them to take ownership of their work and encourage independence. For example, allowing students to choose their own writing topics or giving them multiple prompts to choose from can increase engagement and creativity. Secondly, providing feedback to students is crucial in helping them develop self-regulation skills. Feedback should focus on the process rather than just the product. This means acknowledging the effort students put into their work and providing specific feedback on areas where they can improve. By doing so, students can learn to monitor their own progress and make necessary adjustments to their writing. Thirdly, creating a supportive writing community can help students develop a sense of belonging and foster independence.

This can be done by encouraging peer feedback, collaborative writing, and sharing of writing successes. When students feel supported by their peers and teachers, they are more likely to take risks in their writing and become confident in their abilities. Lastly, it is important to teach students strategies for self-regulation. This includes goal-setting, self-reflection, and self-monitoring. By setting goals, students can have a clear understanding of what they want to achieve and work towards it. Self-reflection allows students to assess their own writing and identify areas for improvement. Self-monitoring helps students stay on track and make adjustments as needed. In my opinion, these strategies are essential for helping students become independent and self-regulated writers. By providing choices, feedback, and creating a supportive community, students can develop the skills and confidence they need to succeed in writing. Moreover, teaching self-regulation strategies can help students become more aware of their own learning process and take control of their own learning.

Chapter 8: Cultural Context and Diversity

The Role of Culture in Child Development

As a psychologist, I believe that culture plays a crucial role in the development of children. Culture shapes children's behavior, attitudes, beliefs, and values, and it provides them with a framework for understanding the world around them. In this article, we will explore the importance of culture in child development and the ways in which it impacts their lives.

Cultural Identity

Cultural identity is an essential part of a child's development. It is shaped by the values, beliefs, and practices of their family, community, and society. Children develop a sense of identity by identifying with the cultural groups to which they belong. They learn the values and beliefs of their culture through interactions with family, friends, and community members. This sense of identity helps children feel a sense of belonging and provides them with a foundation for their social and emotional development.

Language Development

Language is a fundamental aspect of culture, and it plays a significant role in child development. Children learn their native language from their family and community members. The language they speak shapes their worldview, and it provides them with a framework for understanding the world around them. Language also enables children to communicate with others, express their thoughts and feelings, and form relationships. Children who grow up bilingual have an added advantage, as they are exposed to multiple cultures and have a broader perspective on the world.

Values and Beliefs

Culture shapes children's values and beliefs, which play a critical role in their moral development. Children learn what is right and wrong from their family and community members. They are taught the values and beliefs that are important to their culture, such as respect for elders, obedience to authority, and the importance of family.

These values and beliefs help children develop a moral compass and guide their behavior as they grow up.

Socialization

Culture provides a framework for socialization, which is the process through which children learn the norms and values of their society. Children learn how to behave in different situations, how to interact with others, and how to form relationships. Socialization is essential for children's development, as it teaches them how to navigate the world around them and prepares them for adulthood.

Cultural Diversity

Cultural diversity is an important aspect of child development. Children who are exposed to different cultures learn to appreciate and respect cultural differences. They develop a broader perspective on the world and are better equipped to navigate different social and cultural environments. Cultural diversity also helps children develop social skills, such as empathy and understanding, which are essential for building positive relationships with others.

Conclusion

Culture plays a crucial role in child development, shaping children's identity, language development, values and beliefs, socialization, and understanding of cultural diversity. As a psychologist, I believe that it is essential to promote cultural awareness and sensitivity in the way we interact with children. By doing so, we can help children develop a positive sense of identity, appreciate cultural differences, and navigate different social and cultural environments.

Understanding Diversity

As a psychologist, it's important to understand diversity and its impact on individuals and society as a whole. Diversity includes differences in race, ethnicity, gender identity, sexual orientation, age, ability, religion, and socio-economic status. By embracing diversity, we can create a more inclusive and tolerant society.

The Importance of Diversity

Diversity is essential for creating a vibrant and dynamic society. It brings together different perspectives, experiences, and ideas, which can lead to innovation and creativity. Additionally, diversity can help us to break down stereotypes and prejudices, promoting understanding and empathy for those who are different from us.

The Challenges of Diversity

While diversity can be a source of strength, it can also be a source of conflict and tension. People may feel uncomfortable or threatened when they encounter someone who is different from them. Additionally, discrimination and prejudice can prevent individuals from fully participating in society, leading to social and economic disparities.

The Role of Psychology

Psychology plays a crucial role in understanding and addressing the challenges of diversity. Psychologists can study the ways in which diversity affects individuals and communities, and develop interventions to promote tolerance and understanding. Additionally, psychologists can work with individuals and groups to reduce prejudice and discrimination, and promote social justice.

My Opinion

As a psychologist, I believe that embracing diversity is essential for creating a more just and equitable society. By acknowledging and celebrating our differences, we can build a stronger and more inclusive community. It's important to recognize that diversity isn't just a buzzword - it's a fundamental aspect of who we are as human beings.

While there are certainly challenges associated with diversity, I believe that these challenges can be overcome through education, understanding, and empathy. By working together, we can create a world where diversity is not only accepted but celebrated.

Cultural Differences in Parenting Styles

As a psychologist, I believe that parenting styles vary from culture to culture. Each culture has its own beliefs, values, and customs that shape their parenting practices. Understanding these differences is crucial in creating effective parenting strategies that are culturally sensitive and respectful.

Authoritarian Parenting

One of the most common parenting styles is authoritarian parenting. This style is characterized by strict rules, high demands, and low responsiveness. In cultures where hierarchy and obedience are highly valued, such as Asian and Middle Eastern cultures, authoritarian parenting is more prevalent. Parents in these cultures believe that strict rules and discipline will lead to a successful and obedient child.

Permissive Parenting

Permissive parenting is another parenting style that is more prevalent in Western cultures. This style is characterized by low demands, high responsiveness, and little structure. Parents in these cultures value autonomy and independence, and believe that children should be allowed to make their own decisions. This parenting style can lead to children who are confident and independent, but may also lack self-discipline and respect for authority.

Authoritative Parenting

Authoritative parenting is a balanced parenting style that is characterized by high demands, high responsiveness, and clear boundaries. This style is more prevalent in Western cultures, particularly in the United States. Parents in these cultures value communication and collaboration with their children, and believe that clear rules and expectations can be combined with empathy and warmth. This parenting style can lead to children who are self-reliant, responsible, and socially competent.

Conclusion

It is important to note that these parenting styles are not exclusive to specific cultures, and that individual families within a culture may also have their own unique parenting style. Nevertheless, understanding the cultural context in which parenting practices are developed is crucial in creating effective parenting strategies. By recognizing and respecting cultural differences in parenting, we can create a more inclusive and diverse society that values all parenting styles.

My opinion on the matter is that it is important to recognize and respect cultural differences in parenting styles. Every culture has its own unique values and beliefs, and these beliefs shape the way parents raise their children. While some parenting styles may be more effective in certain situations, it is important to understand that there is no "one-size-fits-all" approach to parenting. As psychologists, we can help parents develop strategies that are sensitive to their cultural background, while still promoting positive child development.

Chapter: Creating a Culturally Responsive Environment

As a psychologist, I believe that creating a culturally responsive environment is crucial for ensuring that individuals from diverse backgrounds feel welcomed and supported. A culturally responsive environment acknowledges and values the different cultures, languages, and backgrounds of all individuals, promoting inclusivity and equity. One way to create a culturally responsive environment is by designing the physical space in a way that reflects the diversity of the community. This can be achieved by using artwork, decorations, and posters that celebrate different cultures and traditions. For example, a school can display flags from different countries to recognize the diversity of its student body. Another important aspect of a culturally responsive environment is the language used. Using inclusive language that acknowledges and respects the diverse identities of individuals can create a more welcoming and supportive environment. It is important to use gender-neutral language, avoid cultural stereotypes, and use appropriate terminology when referring to different cultures and communities. In addition to physical space and language, curriculum and instruction also play a vital role in creating a culturally responsive environment. The curriculum should be reflective of the diversity of the community, incorporating materials and resources that represent different cultures and perspectives. It is important to avoid a Eurocentric or Western-centric curriculum and include contributions from various cultures and communities. Moreover, creating a safe and inclusive environment requires building strong relationships with families and communities. Parents and families should be involved in decision-making processes and encouraged to participate in school activities. This can be achieved by having a multicultural parent-teacher organization or hosting events that celebrate diversity and inclusion. In conclusion, as a psychologist, I firmly believe that creating a culturally responsive environment is essential for promoting inclusivity and equity. It involves designing physical space, using inclusive language, incorporating diverse perspectives in the curriculum, and building relationships with families and communities. By doing so, we can create a supportive and welcoming environment for individuals from all backgrounds.

- **Summary of Chapter 8**

As a psychologist, in this chapter, we will discuss the essential elements of writing settings, including the importance of creating a **vivid and immersive environment**, how to effectively use **sensory details** to engage the reader, and how to balance **description with action**. Creating a **vivid and immersive environment** is crucial to transporting the reader into the world of the story. One effective way to do this is through the use of **sensory details**.

Chapter 9: Applying Vygotsky's Theory in the Real World

How to Implement Vygotsky's Ideas at Home

As a psychologist, I believe that Lev Vygotsky's sociocultural theory can provide a wealth of insights into how parents can support their children's cognitive and social development. By emphasizing the importance of social interactions and the role of language in learning, Vygotsky's theory can inform parenting practices that promote children's growth and success. Here are some practical ways to implement Vygotsky's ideas at home: Encourage Collaborative Learning According to Vygotsky, learning occurs through social interactions and collaboration with others. Parents can facilitate this process by encouraging their children to work together on tasks and projects. For example, parents can assign a group project to their children or encourage them to help each other with homework. By working together, children can learn from each other's strengths and weaknesses, and develop important social skills like communication and cooperation. Provide Scaffolding Support Vygotsky introduced the concept of scaffolding, which refers to the temporary support that an adult provides to help a child learn a new task. As a parent, you can provide scaffolding support by breaking down complex tasks into smaller, more manageable steps, and then gradually reducing your involvement as your child becomes more competent. For example, if your child is learning to tie their shoes, you can start by showing them how to tie a knot, and then gradually reduce your guidance until they can do it independently. Use Language to Support Learning Vygotsky believed that language is a critical tool for learning, and that children's language development is closely tied to their cognitive development. Parents can support their children's learning by using language to explain concepts and provide feedback. For example, if your child is struggling with a math problem, you can use language to guide them through the steps and help them understand the underlying concepts. Additionally, by engaging in conversations with your children, you can help them develop their language skills and expand their vocabulary. Provide Meaningful Learning Opportunities According to Vygotsky, learning is most effective when it is relevant and meaningful to the learner. Parents can provide meaningful learning opportunities by encouraging their children to pursue their interests and passions. For example, if your child is interested in science, you can provide them with books, videos, and hands-on activities that allow them to explore and learn about science topics that interest them. In conclusion, Vygotsky's sociocultural theory provides valuable insights into how parents can support their children's cognitive and social development. By encouraging collaborative learning, providing scaffolding support, using language to support learning, and providing meaningful learning opportunities, parents can help their children reach their full potential. So, as a psychologist, I encourage parents to incorporate Vygotsky's ideas into their parenting practices to help their children thrive.

Challenges and Limitations of Applying Vygotsky's Theory

As a psychologist, it's important to recognize that Vygotsky's theory of sociocultural development has had a significant impact on our understanding of cognitive development. However, applying this theory in practice can pose several challenges and limitations.

The Role of Culture

One of the main challenges of applying Vygotsky's theory is understanding the role of culture in cognitive development. Vygotsky believed that culture plays a critical role in shaping our thinking and that learning is a social process that occurs through interaction with others. While this is certainly true, it can be difficult to apply this theory in practice, particularly in cultures where individualism is emphasized over collectivism.

Furthermore, Vygotsky's theory assumes that all cultures are equal in their ability to promote cognitive development. However, this may not be the case, as some cultures may have more resources or opportunities for learning than others. As a psychologist, it's important to consider these factors when applying Vygotsky's theory in practice.

The Zone of Proximal Development

Another limitation of Vygotsky's theory is the concept of the zone of proximal development (ZPD). The ZPD refers to the gap between what a learner can do independently and what they can do with guidance from a more knowledgeable other. While this concept has been widely used in educational settings to promote learning, it can be difficult to determine where a learner's ZPD lies.

Additionally, the ZPD assumes that learners will always progress through this zone with the help of a more knowledgeable other. However, this may not always be the case, as learners may become stuck or may not be motivated to continue learning.

The Role of Language

Vygotsky believed that language plays a critical role in cognitive development, as it allows learners to communicate with others and to internalize knowledge. However, this view has been criticized for being too focused on verbal communication and for not taking into account other forms of communication, such as nonverbal communication or visual aids.

Furthermore, Vygotsky's theory assumes that all learners have equal access to language and that language is a neutral tool that can be used to promote learning. However, this may not be the case, as learners from different linguistic backgrounds may face barriers to learning due to language differences or language biases in educational materials.

Conclusion

Despite these challenges and limitations, Vygotsky's theory remains an important contribution to our understanding of cognitive development. As psychologists, we can use this theory to guide our practice and to promote learning and development in a variety of settings. However, we must also be aware of the limitations of this theory and be willing to adapt our practices to meet the unique needs of each learner.

Success Stories and Case Studies Applying Vygotsky's Theory in the Real World Writing Settings

As a psychologist, I have come across numerous success stories and case studies applying Vygotsky's theory in the real world writing settings. Vygotsky's sociocultural theory emphasizes the importance of social interactions and cultural contexts in shaping human development. This theory has been extensively applied in various educational settings to enhance students' learning experiences and outcomes.

Peer Learning

Vygotsky's theory highlights the importance of peer learning in cognitive development. A successful implementation of this theory is evident in a study conducted by the National Reading Panel (NRP). The study found that students who participated in peer-assisted learning programs showed significant improvement in their reading skills compared to students who did not participate in these programs.

My opinion on this is that peer learning is an effective strategy in enhancing students' learning experiences. It not only promotes social interactions but also provides students with opportunities to actively engage in the learning process. Students who work collaboratively can also exchange ideas, clarify their doubts, and provide constructive feedback, which can facilitate their cognitive development.

Zone of Proximal Development (ZPD)

Vygotsky's theory also emphasizes the importance of the zone of proximal development (ZPD), which refers to the gap between what a learner can do independently and what they can achieve with the assistance of a more knowledgeable other. An effective application of this theory is evident in a study conducted by Medina et al. (2017). The study found that students who received peer-assisted tutoring in writing showed significant improvement in their writing skills compared to students who did not receive this intervention.

My opinion on this is that the ZPD is an essential concept in enhancing students' learning experiences. Teachers or peers who provide appropriate support and scaffolding can help students to achieve their full potential. This can not only enhance students' learning outcomes but also boost their self-efficacy and motivation.

Cultural Contexts

Vygotsky's theory also emphasizes the importance of cultural contexts in shaping human development. An effective application of this theory is evident in a study conducted by Nguyen and Nguyen (2018). The study found that incorporating students' cultural backgrounds and experiences into the writing curriculum can enhance their writing skills and motivation.

My opinion on this is that cultural contexts play a crucial role in shaping students' learning experiences and outcomes. Teachers who incorporate diverse cultural perspectives and experiences into their teaching practices can promote students' sense of belonging, foster their cultural competence, and enhance their motivation and engagement in learning.

Conclusion

In conclusion, Vygotsky's sociocultural theory has been extensively applied in various educational settings to enhance students' learning experiences and outcomes. Peer learning, ZPD, and cultural contexts are some of the key concepts of this theory that have been successfully applied in real-world writing settings. These applications can not only enhance students' learning outcomes but also promote their motivation, engagement, and sense of belonging in the learning community.

Summarize the chapter "Applying Vygotsky's Theory in the Real World Writing Settings"

As a psychologist, I can summarize the chapter "Applying Vygotsky's Theory in the Real World Writing Settings" in the following highlights:

Vygotsky's Theory in Brief

Firstly, Lev Vygotsky was a Soviet psychologist who developed the sociocultural theory of cognitive development. This theory emphasizes the role of social interaction in learning and suggests that language is a tool for thinking and communication. In this view, children learn and develop by interacting with more knowledgeable individuals, who provide guidance and support through a process called scaffolding.

Vygotsky's Theory in Writing Settings

Secondly, Vygotsky's theory has important implications for writing instruction. According to this theory, writing is a socially mediated activity that involves both cognitive and social processes. Therefore, effective writing instruction should provide opportunities for students to interact with peers, teachers, and other experts in writing. In this way, students can receive feedback, learn from others' experiences, and develop their writing skills through collaboration.

Applying Vygotsky's Theory in the Classroom

Thirdly, there are several ways to apply Vygotsky's theory in the classroom. For example, teachers can use scaffolding techniques to support students' writing development. This might involve providing prompts, asking questions, or modeling effective writing strategies. Additionally, teachers can incorporate peer feedback and revision into their writing instruction, creating opportunities for students to interact and learn from one another.

Benefits of Applying Vygotsky's Theory in Writing Settings

Lastly, there are many benefits to applying Vygotsky's theory in writing settings. By emphasizing the social nature of writing, teachers can help students feel more connected to the writing process and improve their motivation to write. Additionally, by providing opportunities for interaction and collaboration, students can learn from one another and develop more complex and nuanced understandings of writing. Overall, Vygotsky's theory provides a powerful framework for effective writing instruction that emphasizes the importance of social interaction and collaboration in the learning process. In my opinion, Vygotsky's theory provides a valuable perspective on learning and development that is especially relevant to writing instruction. By emphasizing the social nature of writing, teachers can help students develop stronger connections to the writing process and improve their writing skills through collaboration and interaction. Therefore, applying Vygotsky's theory in the classroom can lead to more effective and engaging writing instruction that benefits students' learning and development.

Chapter 10: Future Directions and Conclusion

As a psychologist, it is fascinating to observe the emerging research in child development. In recent years, researchers have made significant strides in understanding how children grow and develop, both physically and mentally. Here are some of the most exciting topics that are currently being explored in the field.

Language Development

One of the most crucial areas of child development is language acquisition. Researchers are studying how children learn language and the factors that can affect their progress. For example, recent studies have shown that children who grow up in bilingual households can have better cognitive abilities and executive function than monolingual children. As a psychologist, I believe that it is essential to encourage parents to expose their children to different languages and cultures from a young age. This exposure can help children develop more significant cognitive flexibility, which can benefit them in their personal and professional lives.

Social and Emotional Development

Another critical area of child development is social and emotional growth. Researchers are studying how children develop their emotional intelligence, empathy, and social skills. Studies have shown that children who develop these skills early in life tend to have better mental health and are more successful in their relationships and careers later on. As a psychologist, I believe that parents and caregivers can play a significant role in fostering children's social and emotional development. By modeling positive behavior and providing a nurturing environment, parents can help their children develop the skills they need to succeed in life.

Technology and Development

In today's digital age, children are growing up surrounded by technology. Researchers are studying how this exposure to technology affects children's cognitive, social, and emotional development. Some studies have shown that excessive screen time can have negative effects on children's attention spans and social skills. As a psychologist, I believe that it is crucial for parents to monitor their children's technology use carefully. While technology can be a valuable tool for learning and entertainment, it is important to balance screen time with other activities, such as reading, playing outside, and spending time with family and friends.

Parenting and Child Development

Finally, researchers are studying the role that parenting plays in children's development. Studies have shown that parenting styles can have a significant impact on children's cognitive, social, and emotional growth. For example, children who grow up in authoritative households tend to have better academic and social outcomes than those who grow up in authoritarian or permissive households. As a psychologist, I believe that it is essential for parents to be aware of their parenting style and its potential impact on their children's development. By providing a nurturing and supportive environment, parents can help their children grow into happy, healthy, and successful adults. In conclusion, the emerging research in child development is shedding new light on how children grow and develop. By studying language development, social and emotional growth, technology, and parenting, researchers are providing valuable insights into how parents and caregivers can help their children thrive. As a psychologist, I am excited to see what new discoveries and breakthroughs will come in the future.

New Ideas and Approaches to Parenting

As a psychologist, I've seen many changes in parenting styles over the years. With advancements in technology and a deeper understanding of child development, parents today have access to a wealth of information that can help them raise happy, healthy children. In this chapter, we will explore some new ideas and approaches to parenting that can be beneficial for both parents and children.

Positive Parenting

Positive parenting is a relatively new approach that focuses on building strong relationships between parents and children. It emphasizes the importance of communication, empathy, and mutual respect. Positive parenting can help reduce problem behavior in children and improve their mental health. It can also make parenting more enjoyable and rewarding for parents.

Mindful Parenting

Mindful parenting is another new approach that has gained popularity in recent years. It involves being present and fully engaged with your child in the moment. Mindful parenting can help reduce stress and anxiety in both parents and children. It can also improve communication, strengthen relationships, and promote emotional regulation.

Gender-Neutral Parenting

Gender-neutral parenting is a relatively new approach that challenges traditional gender roles and stereotypes. It involves raising children without assigning them gender roles or stereotypes based on their biological sex. Gender-neutral parenting can help promote gender equality, reduce gender-based discrimination, and improve children's self-esteem.

Attachment Parenting

Attachment parenting is an approach that emphasizes the importance of developing a strong emotional bond between parents and children. It involves practices such as babywearing, co-sleeping, and responsive feeding. Attachment parenting can help promote secure attachment, reduce stress and anxiety, and improve children's cognitive development.

Conclusion

These are just a few of the many new ideas and approaches to parenting that have emerged in recent years. As a psychologist, I believe that these approaches can be beneficial for both parents and children. However, it's important to remember that every family is different, and what works for one family may not work for another. The key is to find an approach that works best for your family and to be open to new ideas and approaches as they emerge.

Continuing the Legacy of Vygotsky

As a psychologist, I believe that Lev Vygotsky was one of the most influential psychologists of the 20th century. His theories on cognitive development, especially the concept of the Zone of Proximal Development (ZPD), have continued to influence the field of psychology and education. One of the most important contributions of Vygotsky was his emphasis on social interactions and cultural context in shaping cognitive development. According to Vygotsky, learning is a social process that occurs through interactions with more knowledgeable others. These interactions occur within a cultural context that provides the tools and symbols that are necessary for cognitive development. Another important concept introduced by Vygotsky is the ZPD. This is the range of tasks that a learner can perform with the assistance of a more knowledgeable other. Vygotsky argued that the ZPD is a key component of learning and that instruction should be tailored to the learner's current level of development within the ZPD. Vygotsky's ideas have had a significant impact on educational practices. Many educators now recognize the importance of scaffolding instruction to help learners reach their potential within their ZPD. Additionally, Vygotsky's emphasis on cultural context has led to a greater appreciation of the diversity of learners and the importance of acknowledging and incorporating cultural differences into instruction. However, as a psychologist, I also recognize that Vygotsky's theories have been subject to criticism. Some researchers have argued that Vygotsky overemphasized the role of social interactions and cultural context and did not give enough attention to biological factors that influence cognitive development. Others have criticized Vygotsky's concept of the ZPD as being too vague and difficult to operationalize. Despite these criticisms, Vygotsky's legacy continues to influence the field of psychology and education. His ideas have inspired numerous research studies and educational practices that aim to promote cognitive development through social interactions and cultural context. As psychologists, we should continue to build on Vygotsky's ideas and refine our understanding of how social, cultural, and biological factors interact to shape cognitive development.

Reflections on Parenting with Vygotsky's Theory

As a psychologist, I believe that Lev Vygotsky's theory of cognitive development provides valuable insights for parents seeking to support their children's growth and learning. Vygotsky's theory emphasizes the importance of social interaction and cultural context in shaping children's development. Here are some key reflections on parenting with Vygotsky's theory:

Scaffolding

One of Vygotsky's most famous concepts is that of scaffolding. This refers to the idea that a more knowledgeable other (such as a parent, teacher, or peer) can provide support to a learner to help them achieve a task that they would be unable to complete alone. Scaffolding involves breaking down a task into smaller parts and gradually withdrawing support as the learner gains competence. As a parent, you can use scaffolding to support your child's learning in a variety of ways. For example, if your child is struggling with a homework assignment, you can break the task into smaller, more manageable pieces and guide them through each step. As your child gains confidence and competence, you can gradually step back and let them take more responsibility for their own learning.

The Zone of Proximal Development

Another key concept in Vygotsky's theory is the zone of proximal development (ZPD). This refers to the range of tasks that a learner is capable of completing with guidance and support from a more knowledgeable other. The ZPD is not static but changes over time as the learner's skills and knowledge increase. As a parent, it is important to understand your child's ZPD and provide opportunities for them to engage in tasks that are challenging but achievable with support. By doing so, you can help your child develop their skills and knowledge and build their confidence as a learner.

Social Interaction

Vygotsky believed that social interaction is a key driver of cognitive development. He argued that children learn best through interactions with others who are more knowledgeable and skilled than they are. These interactions provide opportunities for children to engage in meaningful dialogue, receive feedback, and learn from others' perspectives. As a parent, you can foster your child's cognitive development by providing opportunities for social interaction. This can include engaging in conversations with your child, reading together, playing games, and participating in community activities. By doing so, you can help your child develop their language and communication skills, build their knowledge and understanding of the world, and develop social and emotional competencies.

Cultural Context

Vygotsky emphasized the importance of cultural context in shaping children's development. He argued that children's learning and development are influenced by the cultural and historical context in which they grow up. This includes the values, beliefs, and practices of their family, community, and society. As a parent, it is important to be aware of the cultural context in which your child is growing up and to be sensitive to the diversity of experiences and perspectives that exist in your community. By doing so, you can help your child develop an appreciation for diversity, build their cultural competencies, and foster their sense of belonging and identity.

Conclusion

In conclusion, Vygotsky's theory of cognitive development provides valuable insights for parents seeking to support their children's growth and learning. By using scaffolding, understanding your child's ZPD, fostering social interaction, and being sensitive to cultural context, you can help your child develop their skills, knowledge, and competencies and build a strong foundation for their future success.

Summary of Chapter

As a psychologist, I have analyzed the Future Directions and Conclusion chapter and found it to be a comprehensive overview of the current state and potential developments in language models. The chapter begins by highlighting the increasing demand for more sophisticated language models that can perform complex tasks, such as translation, summarization, and question-answering. This demand is being driven by the growing volume of data available and the need for more efficient ways to process and analyze it. One of the key areas of focus for future language model development is improving their ability to understand context and nuances of language. This will involve incorporating more advanced natural language processing techniques, such as sentiment analysis and named entity recognition. Another important direction is the development of more specialized language models for specific domains, such as legal or medical language. This will require the creation of more specialized training data and the development of more sophisticated algorithms. There is also a growing interest in exploring the ethical and societal implications of language models. As these models become more powerful, there is a risk that they could be used to manipulate or mislead people. It will be important to develop ethical guidelines and regulatory frameworks to ensure that language models are used in a responsible and transparent way. In conclusion, the chapter emphasizes the need for ongoing research and development in the field of language models. While significant progress has been made in recent years, there is still much to be done to realize their full potential. As a psychologist, I believe that language models have the potential to revolutionize the way we interact with information and each other. However, it will be important to approach their development and use with caution and responsibility.

Printed in Great Britain
by Amazon